Petrichor

Other books by Adam Hughes

Pilgrim Poems (Pudding House, 2010)

Petrichor

Adam Hughes

The New York Quarterly Foundation, Inc.
New York, New York

NYQ Books™ is an imprint of The New York Quarterly Foundation, Inc.

The New York Quarterly Foundation, Inc.
P. O. Box 2015
Old Chelsea Station
New York, NY 10113

www.nyqbooks.org

Copyright © 2010 by Adam Hughes

All rights reserved. No part of this book may be used or reproduced in any manner whatsoever without written permission of the author. This book is a work of fiction. Any references to historical events, real people or real locales are used fictitiously. Other names, characters, places, and incidents are products of the author's imagination, and any resemblance to actual events or locales or persons, living or dead, is entirely coincidental.

First Edition

Set in New Baskerville

Layout and Design by Raymond P. Hammond
Cover Illustration: "Trees in Fog, VA" ©1996 Mel Curtis | www.melcurtis.com

Library of Congress Control Number: 2010938557

ISBN: 978-1-935520-35-1

Petrichor

Acknowledgments

"Caricature" and "Variations on a Theme by Gregory Nazianzen" appeared in the September 2009 issue of *The Houston Literary Review*. "Streaking in the Garden of Gethsemane" appeared in the December 2009 issue of *The Houston Literary Review*.

"Tenebrae" appeared in the September 2009 issue of *Flutter*. "Assiniboin Dead Perched in Boughs of Lodgepole Pine" appeared in the November 2009 issue of *Flutter*. "Stars Are Pretty" appeared in the January 2010 issue of *Flutter*. "Sans" appeared in the March 2010 issue of *Flutter*.

"Where, Oh Death" appeared in the Fall 2009 issue and "Dear Thief" appeared in the Fall 2010 issue of the *Boston Literary Magazine*.

"Upon Hearing a Train" and "When Bonhoeffer Hung Naked" appeared in issue #105 of *Gloom Cupboard*.

"Poem on a Polaroid" was published by Silenced Press in September 2009.

"Your First Breath" was published by *Errant Parent* in November 2009.

"Standing Atop Mt. Pleasant, August 26, 2009" appeared in the December 2009 issue of *The Foliate Oak*.

"A Moby Dick Kind of Sadness" appeared in the Winter 2010 issue of *tinfoildresses*.

"Sitting on the Deck with Ranger Rick", "The Mist Beneath Eagle's Rock", and "The Poet Identifies Beauty" appeared in the January 2010 issue of *Leaf Garden*.

"God Speaks of Time" and "How to Swim in a Cenote" appeared in the February 2009 issue of *Writers' Bloc*.

"To My Grandfather (1931-2008)" appeared in the Spring 2010 issue of *WestWard Quarterly*.

"A Prayer for Peace" and "Kuka'ilimoku" were accepted for publication in the *New York Quarterly*.

"A Moby Dick Kind of Sadness," "Barrier Islands," "Centralia, PA," "Dispatches from Surtsey," "For Jules," "Here There Be Dragons," "How to Swim in a Cenote," "Inscribed in Cloudbank Vapor Over a South Sea Island," "Inside the Chu Pong Massif," "Instructions Before Beginning a Journey," "It Was Me," "Lullaby," "Mapping the Eschaton," "Night in the Uncharted Territories," "Peregrinatio," "Poems Written on Leaves," "Silage," "Stars Are Pretty," "The Chemical Properties of Snow," "The Gong Doesn't Sound Too Bad," "The Ingredients of Lake Air," "Traveling to Banzakar," "Variations on a Theme by Gregory Nazianzen," "When We're Older We'll Buy a Cottage in Lakeside," and "Woodwose" all appeared in the chapbook, *Pilgrim Poems* (Pudding House, 2010).

For Grandpa,
who was a poet without ever writing a line

always my hero, my mentor, my guide

Contents

Final Instructions Before Beginning a Journey / 15
Peregrinatio / 16
Blame the Welsh / 17
Omphalos / 18
Traveling to Banzakar / 19
Poem on a Polaroid / 22
It Was Me / 23
Beneath the Belly of a Horse / 24
Petrichor / 25
God Speaks of Time / 26
Woodwose / 27
Owl Pellets at Wahkeena Nature Preserve / 28
Before a Gaza Sunrise / 29
Banzakarian Hymns / 30
For Jules / 32
Here There Be Dragons / 33
Maundy Thursday, 1968 / 34
My Father-in-Law Who Has Tasted Dog / 35
Skellig Hymn / 36
The Sisters' New Stairs / 37
Caricature / 38
Silage / 39
Bones / 40
Inscribed in Cloudbank Vapor Over a South Sea Island / 41
Learning to Swim / 43
Streaking in the Garden of Gethsemane / 44
To My Grandfather (1931-2008) / 45
Your First Breath / 46

Mapping the Eschaton   / 47
Variations on a Theme by Gregory Nazianzen   / 48
How to Swim in a Cenote   / 50
At Night You Pretend You're Fierce   / 51
Becoming Prayer   / 52
Confession   / 53
The Chemical Properties of Snow   / 54
The Gong Doesn't Sound Too Bad   / 55
God Bless the Lepers   / 57
Dispatches from Surtsey   / 58
On Friday Mornings I Watch Them Take the Trash Away   / 59
On Saturdays I Mow the Grass at Pleasant Hill Cemetery   / 60
Stepping Over Our Bodies   / 65
Speaking For My Grandfather   / 66
Why I Hate Nasal Discharge   / 67
Where, Oh Death   / 68
Wisps of Something More Than Smoke   / 69
Sitting on the Deck With Ranger Rick   / 70
A Moby Dick Kind of Sadness   / 71
The Mist Beneath Eagle's Rock   / 72
Speaking for the Mayan Dead   / 73
Love Poem, Translated From the Banzakarian   / 74
Lakeside   / 75
Dear Thief   / 76
From Off the Western Coast   / 77
Holy of Holies   / 78
In Remembrance of Robert McNamara   / 79
The Poet   / 80
The Poet Identifies Beauty   / 81
Observing a Polynesian Face Tattoo   / 82
Standing Atop Mt. Pleasant, August 26, 2009   / 83
Upon Hearing a Train   / 84

The View from Síocháin Díthreabhach   / 85
Thoughts on Neda From Deer Creek State Park   / 86
Kuka'ilimoku   / 88
Centralia, PA   / 89
Malagasy   / 90
Inside the Chu Pong Massif   / 91
Night in the Uncharted Territories   / 92
The Ingredients of Lake Air   / 94
Eschatologically Speaking   / 95
Habits of Ohio Waterfowl and Fifteen Month Olds   / 97
A Prayer for Peace   / 98
Assiniboin Dead Perched in Boughs of Lodgepole Pine   / 100
Stars are Pretty   / 101
Sans   / 102
Of Ba'al   / 103
When Bonhoeffer Hung Naked   / 105
Poems Written on Leaves   / 106
Joe Inushiak   / 110
Barrier Islands   / 111
Tell My Daughter That One Day I'll Die   / 112
Elegy for a Bengali Island   / 113
The Mound Builders   / 114
Tenebrae   / 116
Squirrel Somewhat Dead   / 117
For My Daughter, Fifteen Months Old   / 118
The Dead of Beaumont Hamel   / 119
Benediction   / 120
When We're Older We'll Buy a Cottage in Lakeside   / 121
Lullaby   / 122

Petrichor

Final Instructions Before Beginning a Journey

> *"Traveller, you must set out*
> *At dawn. And wipe your feet upon*
> *The dog-nose wetness of earth."*
> —Wole Soyinka

I'm leaving when I can see
my hand without squinting.
I'll look far until I see the earth's
roundness; I'll walk until I feel
the eastward slope. I'll stare
at the sun while it's pale and low
and powerless to blind. Winking
through clouds and ridges
topped by birches with bare bone
trunks, this solar top peaks
over Eagle's Rock and promises
psalms. Meet me

near the third ridge from the right
on the eastern horizon.
Follow the river and you'll get there
by May. Get there when the sun
is still losing the battle with dew
and let your feet be bathed
in victorious condensation.

We'll walk until our feet are dry.

Peregrinatio

Come with me, we'll foliage through
tree-herds; we'll climb graveyard ridges, loamed
with bits of skeletal remains; we'll hook our prehensile
hearts around arboreal bulk, interior concentrics
too many to count.

Come with me and dive in dugong meadows,
through popsicle blue currents and past remains
of planes and pilots scattered along the Bimini Road.
We'll rip time and land on Grand Turk alone
on pre-Arawak sands.

Come with me and mau-mau from Kikuyu hills;
we'll whisper sweetness in KiSwahili; we'll rest
on falls-fed shores; we'll crater the Serengeti
and we'll ngorongoro swaying grasses until our hands find
each other's in the serval-spotted night.

Our grotto love, cavernous and damp,
fed by submerged streams, home
to remains of mammoths, where wonders
obsidian away just waiting for illumination.

Blame the Welsh

My non-preacher grandpa
cigaretted himself to death. Addiction
was in his capillaries and was
plasma-passed to me.

I blame the Welsh for my desire to read
the Mabinogi when my friends
were reading their dads' old
Playboys. Instead of centerfolds,
I dreamed of druids incantating
amidst sacred Anglesey oaks.

My great-uncle Dylan Thomased
on St. David's Day. They found
him wearing an old powder blue tux
jacket with no pants and a yellow daffodil
pinned to the lapel.

I fault Wales for making me find
beauty in dying old mining towns. I glimpse
haunting familiarity in Glouster and Shawnee
where my relatives climbed out
of the Ohio and straight into
the mines.

The obsidian shafts of Cardiganshire
and Trimble contain the final
breaths of miners who looked
like me. The wild Cymric places echo
with baritone voices—my grandfather's,
my father's, and my own.
I blame the Welsh for my loving
the wildness and the echo.

Omphalos

When Adam was loamed and dusted,
clayed into manhood, bypassing
umbilical necessity, did Yahweh
reach with galaxial fingers and sculpt
a potemkin navel? Prone above
tectonics in forced migration,
pre-breath, heart unstarted,

silent in mountain-ringed virgin
earth. Did the hands of the Unmoved
Mover accordion these river stone
plains and scrape out canyons
etch-a-sketched with floodlines
and eroded by deific saliva?

Were the rings of Edenic
trees oil on canvas? Watercolor?
Were paleo femurs and ancient
imprints simply the stuff of children's
bedtime stories, Ossian-real?
Was archaeopteryx a lie?

I hope not. I could not worship
a trickster-God, coyoting and giggling
at Adam's gullible children
with their well-earned navels.

Traveling to Banzakar

I.

We'll Traveler the lunar surface,
march through marshes sentried
by cattails, travois the plains
and hitchhike aboard tortoisan glaciers.
We'll seek the gates of Banzakar
in alleyways and highway overpasses
and we'll seek its Easter egg borders
guarded by flaming gnomes
armed with submachine guns.

We'll gypsy through ravines dug
by sheets of retreating ice, fingers
raking now-fecund loam. We'll stop
to ask directions and the gas station attendant
will point toward Mt. Pleasant without
looking up from the *Columbus Dispatch*.
On the sandstone cliff we'll look for signs
and Banzakarian landmarks. Finding
none we'll jump and hope we find it

before impact.

II.

The ground holds no answers.
We shake ourselves rid of needles
from pines and peregrine off
to seek the wave-nibbled shores
of the Vastalose Empire. From there
we'll pass through until we find

Banzakar-of-the-Silent-Glens. Maps
all mothed, we set out guided by
transient stars. We bypass Tír na nÓg

and arrive in Manitoba. Here the stars
smell like rain and we leave with
vapored nostrils. Into daybreak
we walk with eyes blinded by the sun
rising out of Ontario. From sheets
of Greenland ice we find a repository
for lost birds—wing bone of giant auk, beak
of dodo, vestigial feathers plucked
from the carcass of a giant moa.

We're getting close.

III.

East of graveyards holding skaldic bones,
north of darkness, south of polar magnetism,
we finish our meal of reindeer hoof and baby seal.
Picking fur and carotene from teeth long dulled
by kelp, our journey renews. On the double blue
horizon sits the shores of Banzakar. Amid the breakers

we lose it. Boat and Banzakar gone, Vastal beaches
beckon but keep moving like a cloud of fireflies.
We pass through Fiddler's Green, oar-backed
and unquestioned, and exit the city limits through
a hedgerow of bougainvillea and corn shocks.

IV.

Have you been to Banzakar?
Have you found its shores
its gull-guarded piers, anemone
tides, where milk and molasses pours?

If you've seen those salmon-jumped
waters, the bank with a selkie pelt,
remember to light the cabin for me
alone on Orion's Belt.

I'll be there when winter is over
before the land bridge melts away,
so ready a space in the ground for me
where I can warmly stay.

Poem on a Polaroid

I'm two, maybe three,
on a couch of drab
gold, lima bean
green and turd brown.

On my already angular
face is a leprechaun
grin, eyes caught
in mid-gleam beneath

my still-bald scalp. I'm
lifting up my Muppet Babies
shirt, tiny hand beneath,
frozen in polaroid

purgatory—caught in mid
tickle. I always loved
when others' hands
would knead my flesh

into a tub of ticklish
goo. I'd scream for them
to stop and then beg them
to continue. I suppose

I still do. On the
once-white strip in faded
black it reads, "Ad
is easily entertained."

It Was Me

who wrote starbound messages
in crustacean constellations, who spoke
transcontinental currents and warm
water that flows past northern islands
coated in rock and ice. I'm the one
who weaves your sleep-thoughts
and teaches children the language
of fairies and woodland creatures.
I'm the one who ate the fruit
that was freely permissible, but I simply
rubbed it on my sleeve instead of washing
it properly. For shame. I confess—
I am not God, I am not prophet,
I am not shaman or priest,
I am not good medicine or the newest
incarnation of a Buddhist holy man.
I admit, I do not know who I am.
I might be the Mariana Trench, the breath
talk of mourners, the shoulders of sherpas
and the hip of Hebrew patriarchs,
the home water sensing hands of Tongan
navigators and the glazed
eyes of Valhallan dead. Or, just maybe,
I am the meeting of two rivers,
muddy and clear, guilty and innocent,
prisoner and free.

Beneath the Belly of a Horse

Tiny hands grip
a fist-large pommel,
Dad's firm hands leading
the docile pony. Fresh
snow, four inches,
landscape of muffled
sun-bright ice, hoof
and foot prints trailing
back toward the barn.

Saddle-cinch too loose,
passengers sliding. Dad
looks back and sees
daughter and son hanging
like overgrown bats
from the belly of the horse,
silent, hands still gripping
the pommel.

They never said a word;
just hung there like
ice-storm branches.

Petrichor

We ride our bikes around the church, havocing
the earthworms. With blacktop steaming
like the island-birthing ocean, we smell
the puddles and the aroma of evaporation.
                                              We pretend to sail
carved sea canoes beneath open clouds
and above the sea lion surf, circling the shadow
of the steeple. You are my girlfriend until
we forget. Tires skidding on pavement,
                                                these asphalt-dark waters
part for tightening turns and gyres of adolescence,
puffin hatchlings learning to fly. Our beaks
are ungainly. Adrift in this estuary of fallen
things—leaves, drizzle, the feather of a gull—
                                          westing toward the sun,
daring each other to ride down the hill. Terminal
moraine, maze of rocks and grass-covered silt
pocked by groundhog holes, sharing memories
of ice, beckoning us to conquest and bloody knees.
We skraeling these shores and repel invaders
                                              until our stomachs growl
                                              and we go home for dinner.

God Speaks of Time

With the spin of Saturnite rings
and the thup-thup-thup of columbidic
wings, I launch time from the hurricane-
spawning flaps of a monarch butterfly.
This fabergé earth, this present declension,
this conjugating race, a people fascinated
by octaves of light. From Babel
to Stonehenge to Teotihuacán these
drops of deitic vapor have tried to grasp
that which my Andromeda-spinning
fingers have failed to grip. Nothing

is more difficult to catch than
a feral butterfly. Still I weave webs
of digital gossamer, projected
upon the ceiling of heaven. Today
is old and young, Rip Van Winkle
in mid-nap, a new movie I've seen before.
Projection is dangerous, though,

tired eyes mistake clear numeric angles
and the seraphim have been known
to oversleep. I breathe in chronology,
receive the timeless prayers of sinners,
and glance at Heaven's clock with
the only eyes that can read it.

Woodwose

Woodwose these glens guarding
ponds where St. Kevin jumped naked
into nettles. Carry the mud of estuary,
vapor of tidal spray, find the holts
where otters play, dine on salmon
scored by lutran teeth. Don't forget

to mark the trail with bits of fabric
and rye bread. Don't forget to eat
all the crumbs of Jesus and wash down
the Host with the blood of Lindow Man.
From peat-stacked bogs sentried

by Saturn-eyed owlets, offer your prayers
to the High King of Heaven and druid
your nocturnal dreams of liberation
from the Roman Empire.

Owl Pellets at Wahkeena Nature Preserve

Looking through avian
hairballs seemed so cool
in fourth grade. I kept one
for nine years in the top drawer
of my dresser, next to the mask
they used to put me to sleep
before my first surgery. I still smell
long dissipated aromas
of anesthetic and owl
puke. Full of bits of tiny bone
and clumps of mouse-grey
fur, the pellet sat there
unused and unnoticed. Seeing
it reminded me of the stuffed
beaver, the long-dead
skunk on the mantle
and the cage of living owls.
We learned of glacial
migration and wildlife
preservation amidst captive
specimens dead and alive.

I have not seen a live owl
since, but I still have a piece
of cricetidaen spine. I guess
some things just can't
be digested.

Before a Gaza Sunrise

Among ruins of Philistia, Ahmed
opens his falafel stand and worries
about his bottom line—the intifada
is bad for business. If Ismail
was a wild foal then his children
have entered their mustang years.

On this spot where Jacob wrestled
Yahweh, his descendants have not
forgotten who won. Elohim, bested,
cheats and Jacob limps away—
victorious but maimed. Now
where the hip came unsocketed
they eat falafel too.

Refugees and militants patrol
the pre-sun land of ruined mortar.
Stars and crescents wake to walk
the most fought for soil on earth.
Both seek peace; they just can't
agree between Shalom and Salaam.

Banzakarian Hymns

> *"Matuj nexif aziqiz-wij"* [Hope is a vulture]
> —Banzakarian proverb

I. Nomads

Rain smells
different here. From these western
coastlines we watch the ocean
extinguish the sun. Praise
to reignition, praise to the tidal
movements of the warmth-giver,
praise to the sea gods
who return our light
each morning. The skies
return their thanks with gifts
of water for the sea
and we linger long
enough to know that there is peace
between the waters.

II. Mariners

How can we smell
falling water when marine scents
cling to the hair
of our nostrils? Decaying coral
and kelp in bloom, decks
scrubbed by flying fish, the smoky
scent of fish oil tapers all remind
us that ours is a home made
of rain. We flotsam and jetsam,
seabirding these breakers
and dreaming of rocks
and the color green.

III. Monks

A greeting to the still-wet sun,
to the darting, shifting
terns and gulls and the shimmering
fins that hang from their beaks.
We sing of the day
and pray for the night.

IV. Exiles

Rain smells
different here. Asphalt
lends its pungent steam
to the odor of leaded
drops and wisps of smoky
vapor remind us
that we are far offshore.
The stars look different;
we sing our songs and write
our poems beneath
these foreign constellations
and all the while we know
that the vultures are circling.
And we hope.

For Jules

Mountains with white-caps
rising down—a range
of sunken peaks. Here
nautical mountaineers
scale aquatic heights
while valleys lie in obsidian
darkness—unexplored. What good
is a mountain when its majesty
is observed only by impious
crustaceans? Below,
surrounded by evolutionary
oddities—water-breathing
sherpas—summits tower
unnoticed by a race
fascinated with the dry.

Here There Be Dragons

Today we coracle spin
like nest-guarding gulls;

tomorrow we'll break through
the Pillars of Hercules.

Where longships and caravels
disappear into baleenic jaws,

we watch the Atlantic devour
the defenseless sun. Parsing

the winds, we oil-slick in present
perfect. Between the stars we raft

through sedimentary shoals
somewhere northeast of the Sargasso.

The Whale's Way, plankton-full,
hums and groans below our ribs

and we porpoise on, closing
our eyes to the serpents and sailing

beneath the sagging chin
of the tide maker.

Maundy Thursday, 1968

Too bad we weren't
Catholics.

Because then Chris wouldn't
have choked on bread; he
would have choked on Jesus and
we wouldn't have had to do
the Heimlich. Then Chris wouldn't have
spit everything all over
Reverend Mann's new purple scarf
and the elements of grace
would have been undefiled by
scrambled eggs mixed with
butterscotch candies
only partially broken down
by stomach acid.

I don't think Chris ever
took Communion again.
He died an arm-scarred
hippie sometime after
Altamont. I wonder if it's because
Jesus never got past
his epiglottis.

My Father-in-Law Who Has Tasted Dog

He was twenty and
Californian, his
pre-Ohio self, visiting
Tijuana. There he met
a street-side vendor hawking
tacos to hungry American
tourists. He ordered two
and crisped into one.

"These are good,
what kind of meat is this?"

"Doggie."

He didn't eat
the second one.

Now he laughs
when he tells
the story—his eyes
disappearing between
encroaching
eyebrows and overly
aggressive
cheeks. He says
it was a good
taco.

Skellig Hymn

Kittiwakes and guillemots circle
the beehive cells of crescent-haired
anchorites. With feet and knees
scarred from penitential climbing
of Croagh Patrick and Mount Brendan,
they limp and crawl their way
from vespers to nocturn to matins.
Here, white caps leap to lick
the shins of the devout while
fulmars dive in search of sanctified
fish. Praising Triune God,
the pious pray before their rock-hewn
altar and the Lord shows mercy
in the form of sea-fresh herring.

The Sisters' New Stairs

For the carpenter of Loretto Chapel

I come mid one evening, hands of
tools and clothes still smelling
re-entral. Of children ringed,
St. Vitus dancing, ashes
of porcelain and compressed clay;
I thought of sisters well-watering
the plants out front and stairwelling
rickety cliffs to sing the praises
of the one who hears all climbers' songs.
Old Santa Fe Trail, highwayed,
blacktop wagon ruts and ox-hoof skid marks,
I followed it lumbered down with foreign wood.

I hear you now, modern man. *"It was
spruce!"* Of course spruce.
What did you expect? Lebanon cedars?
Heaven-grown timber barked with glory
and Eden clothes? A true cross beam,
still holed from centurion nails? Spruce is practical.

Of course it's centrally supported.
Free-standing planks are like moons
without gravity—luning all over deep space,
colliding with rocks and comets
and nova remnants. No miracle, no lifetime
warranty. They asked me nothing permanent,
nothing miraculan, nothing encoded
with mitochondrial divinity. Just steps
to reach the belfry. I got them belfry-far.
That's as high as I go.

Caricature

I was a twelve
year old origami
swan. We stopped
in front of the artist
slouched on a stool
at his booth at
Cedar Point.
I wanted nothing
more than to have him
sketch my picture.
Thirty dollars and I
sat statued for twenty
minutes.

Teeth that fell somewhere
between Bobby Kennedy
and Bugs Bunny—beavers
were jealous.
My ears were mule
big and car-door
open. The bronze
arrowhead necklace
prominent beneath
my hairless, pointless
chin. My parents
and the seagulls
laughed.
I did not.

The picture is long
gone now—my teeth
and wide ears
remain. But
that sketch
wasn't me.

Silage

Today I found, beneath the highway overpass,
an empty canvas backpack,
a sheet of notebook paper,
a bicycle tire,
three chewed-up tennis balls,
a size eleven men's Reebok,
and a dead bird of indistinguishable classification.
It might have been a wren.

Today I found, beneath the railroad bridge,
an empty propane tank,
a wrinkled-wet library copy of "The Prophet",
the iridescence of a peacock feather, peacock missing,
and the odor of an adolescent skunk ape.

Today I found, beneath the shade of a slippery elm,
a nomad yurt, covered by the hide of a Przewalski's horse,
the sand from a Gobi storm,
a pinch of the ashes of Troy,
the spirit of Albert Camus,
a Seychelle seashell,
and there I found

that the bird was definitely a wren.

Bones

My senior year I wore
the number one, not because
I was the best, but because it was
the only number that would
fit on my back. I tried thirty-three
but the rounded parts wrapped
around my side and ribs and reminded
everyone that I was a dribbling
skeleton, hugged
by double digits.

Inscribed in Cloudbank Vapor Over a South Sea Island

We yurt-skins, we birchbark roofs, we rafters
of oak and cedar, we who watch from overhead
and guard the powdered scalps of newborns

We kingdoms, we phyla, we genera and species,
we who divide and classify, sorting by
mechanisms of heating and cooling

We curragh hides, we ancient mariners,
we who plot our course by foreign suns,
we who are denied entry into Tír na nÓg

We taro, we manioc, we sugar cane,
we who stockpile mana and navigate
waters by touch, recognizing home by the warmth
of amniotic seas

We lunar gods, we Gog and Magog,
we tops of ziggurats, we who sacrifice
our firstborn sons and spare the ram

We hamstrings of wallabies, we bone
of cassowary crests, we who sing
the Dreamtime and paint our rocks
with mouth-held chalk

We tremor lips, we kestrel eyes,
we *anthropos*, we *ekklesia*,
we who stand on glaciered heights
and calve the ice from frozen altars

We pollinated winds, we sacred
directions, we kivas opening
to the fourth world, we who dance
with snakes and pray for the scent
of approaching rain

We pilgrims almost home, we killdeer
guarding beach-gravel eggs, we dancing
beneath this pantheon, this floor
beneath the feet of God.

Learning to Swim

Miniature arms and legs, body
made for speed and endurance;
awkward on land, at home in
shallow water—a lanky, skinny
pinniped. Bathtub olympian,
Mark Spitz of the home
hygiene station, ear-scars
still healing, hearing gone, career
derailed. Nine times under
anesthesia, inner ear exposed, still
in the pool on family vacations.

Lessons at the YMCA—an ugly
duckling, twelve years old
in a class of five-year-olds.
I cried on the side of the pool
and the kid next to me asked
if I was a mouse or a man. I
pushed him in and went home.

My wife has made it her life's
mission to take this terrestrial
body and teach it aquatic
secrets. But I won't
float. I look at my feet and
sink like one acquitted of
charges of witchcraft—innocent
but drowning. Now I only
wade in de-populated pools,
solitary in my inability to
cut through the water like
a monk seal. I make my
confession and people look
at me like one who's never
tasted chocolate.

Streaking in the Garden of Gethsemane

I run

like Joseph before Potiphar's
wife. I leave my clothes in their
accusing hands, skin now open
to thorn assault. Through olive
groves I glimpse torch-light
swaying like temple prostitutes
before the fires of Ba'al. Gentile

might displayed at the cost
of an ear, soon replaced, sword
scabbard-sheathed. What could
I have done against the imperial
eagle? His eyes practically begged
me to flee. So through the veiled
night and the Kidron

I run.

To My Grandfather (1931-2008)

I saw a tree in the woods today;
it reminded me of you:
a towering trunk of white oak leaning
like the mast on a foundering ship.
I wondered at its former grandeur,
when it was a model of deciduosity,
a leafy bastion impregnable
above the forest floor.
I pictured it a primal landmark
for some poor wayward traveler—
a land-locked lighthouse
rescuing the lost.

But the tower has been taken
and Alaric is at the gates.
The once-proud child of Spring
is now withered and angled
and covered with slimy moss—
reclining yet unbroken.

A light-less beacon it remains
for those who dwell nearby,
no matter that those time-aged limbs
no longer touch the sky.

Your First Breath

Amniotic exhale,
shock of open air on
quickly drying skin,
placental home left
behind in favor of life
outside uterine walls.

I had spent the last
hour and a half staring
at the imperial crown
of your head, wondering
if the rest of you
would be the color
of communion wine.
But I missed

your first post-natal
moments because I was busy
throwing up.

Mapping the Eschaton

Morning curtains hang
from rods of cumulus and evaporated
sea. The coastline smells of recent rain
and cryptids and the stars seek darker
grounds. I'm a Tsimshian mask colored
with shades of ocean inlet, fire, and ash,
with eyes of chipped baleen; beak and gaze
as empty as salmon nets on dammed
rivers. I'm unkempt,
like the thatched roof hair
of feral children. I'll potlatch
my possessions and still spend
the night alone. The colder the night,
the brighter the stars.

Tonight I'll give up
the study of war. Tonight I'll find
where the Kushtaka sleep. Tonight
I'll spear my demons, jinns, and ghosts.
Tonight I'll chart these sounds and coves
until I know exactly where I've been.
The odor of downpour lingers
and I have found the afterlife.

Variations on a Theme by Gregory Nazianzen

for Ron Adkins

*"I know we are as though making a great voyage on a raft,
or hastening towards the starry sky upon small wings"*
—Gregory Nazianzen

I.
In the obsidian ocean
depths, we waited
for salvation. Instead we found lots
of zooplankton. Above, Jasconius
waited like a giant
warm-blooded taxi
and so we floated
to the surface like so many
pieces of cork—buoyant
and full of holes.

II.
This oar is getting heavy.
And still no one has asked me
what it is I'm
carrying. Damned
danceless ghouls pulling at
this inland mariner.

III.
I wonder what happened
to Henry Hudson. Sailing
rowboat-bound adrift in
fly-boat wake;
what good is a name-
sake if it becomes
a tomb?

IV.
Today my daughter
smiled at me while drinking
her mother's milk. She
starts butternut squash
next week. Enamel
appears out of
gums like Surtsey
out of the North Atlantic
but she remains
six-months
bald.

How to Swim in a Cenote

First, dive into mouthwash
blue waters, feel the coolness
of subterranean tides. Float
past sacrificial bowls, headless

chicken skeletons and bones
of captives sent into
diverless depths. Hands on
guideline, remember that

touch is more important
than sight. Through flooded
caverns, water blurs—beware
these halocline depths that smell

of sulfur. Here, what once
was fresh is now seasoned with
ancient sea-salt. If you find
your way out, climb from

this Yucatan well and gaze
on its leaf-enshrouded
mouth. Beneath a hole
in Chichen Itza, Hunahpu

awaits your sacrifice.
Toss in a Timex
for safe travel;
it descends to aquatic

abyss through blended
waters and Xibalban
shadow.

At Night You Pretend You're Fierce

When it's too dark
to sit outside, I tickle
you and make
faces. Your eyes
squint into Eskimo
orbs and your nose
scrunches and flares
while your tiny
mouth opens to
eat me. I see your
twin peaks emerging
from gum-line ridges.

You puff air through
your nose, arms
swinging and feet
kicking. You're
a moth with owl-eyed
wings—optically

fierce one moment, huffing
autonomy, the next those
hazel irises lid-covered
and your breathing
deep—back into
your cocoon of sleep.

Becoming Prayer

> *"Our whole life, every act and gesture, even a smile must become a hymn of adoration, an offering, a prayer. We must become prayer—prayer incarnate."*   —Paul Evdokimov

Today I strip
away my layer of
God-touched clay.
I remove my bones
and deconstruct
epistemology.
I break down
the Saturnite rings
and I cease my mothing
around extra-solar
lighting. From Gnostic
shores I punt the coast
and raise my Jonah
sails. I'll not stop
until I'm naked and halfway
to Tarshish. From those
unstilled waves I'll
swim until I find
resurrection and reset
my theosis. Only then
will I accept the new
garment and eat
of the fattened calf.
Once full I'll exhale
doxology and call it
good.

Confession

Forgive me.
I pulled the cord
in the hospital men's room—
the one that said "pull
if you need help."

I didn't need help
but it was tantalizing
like Bathsheba's bathed and oiled
hair. And I was
weak.

The Chemical Properties of Snow

After a snowfall there is no
smell. Odorless air so recently full
of flakes falling from volcanic ash
skies, now clear and sunny
and scentless. Life is figuring out
what precipitation leaves behind.

I was thirteen, looking at an old
issue of National Geographic. I fell
in love with the eyes of Afghan Girl
and imagined that all refugees
had coral sea eyes and pure, though dirty,
skin. I looked for her in Gaza
but everyone there had ugly eyes.

Maybe snow smells
like the dirt from the bridge
of her nose. The fennec fox
has giant ears; so do the heads
of Easter Island. Neither has anything to do
with snow and both smell
like a mix of camel spit and sweet potato.

I wish I still spoke the ancient language
of ten-month-olds. If I did
I'd figure out the aroma of flakes
of taro and solve the enigmas of Atlantis
and the Soviet Union. But I guess life is about

mysteries—like whether God blinks
and why barnacles exist
and what happens to frozen petrichor
when it thaws.

The Gong Doesn't Sound Too Bad

I could mine the wind for Salish verbs
and read Kwakiutl love poetry to the skull
of D. B. Cooper; but if he does not respond
I am merely a barking otter.

I could decode the Long Count calendar
and predict a polar shift; but if I am wrong
then no one will listen to me about
the chupacabras.

I could choose the grass less trampled
and the trail less wagon-rutted; but if those
who follow are ambushed by Arapaho
then I probably shouldn't go back east.

I could cry salt-free tears to cut back
on sodium and I could lift stones next
to Magnus Ver Magnusson; but if I stare
at my reflection like Bambi in a stream
then I am nothing but a big guy
holding a rock.

I could go to Tara and be named
Ard Rí, and I could find Fionn's trumpet
and wake the Fianna; but if I sleep
with Oisin's wife, I should eat
the blackened biscuit.

I could sail a balsa raft to prove
that South America was discovered
by Maori fishermen; but if I get
a face tattoo I won't be invited to Thanksgiving.

I could yell "Freedom!" from the wrack
and spill haggis on my kilt; but if I paint
my face woad-blue, I will probably
get cancer.

I could find subterranean rivers
and name them after you, but if my
gestures remain underground then I
should probably just marry one of those
blind albino scorpions—they sting
a bit but couldn't care less if I
don't keep up with the laundry.

God Bless the Lepers

God bless the lepers—
who strut and fret their hour;
who tiller vessels into sandbars,
sail puntless keelboats;
who orca unsuspecting pinnipeds;
who troubadour the coasts of Horse Latitude atolls;
who atlatl cylindrical dreams
and spears made from branches
of ornamental pear;
who Viking their neighbors
and Hitler strangers; who eunuch
statues of Hermes and sleep with Spartan queens;
whose women produce condensed milk;
who barnacle to wharf-wood;
who stalk mushrooms through cloudy
forests; who pluck May apples and mix
their venom leaves with sprigs of baby's breath
to flank the cross upon the altar;
who whisper doxology from Kalaupapa
cliffs; who wrestle with angels
and minotaurs and bridge-covered trolls;
who Bedouin from dune peak to mirage and back;
whose dandruff-skin falls
like Himalayan flurries; who wait
outside the city gates; whose nimbus
circled faces drop pyre pile ashes;
who swim in seraphim-stirred waters
and look to you with Dead Sea eyes.

Dispatches from Surtsey

I.
Vomiting
molten core—seasick
and spewing
solid ground
in the north Atlantic.

II.
Surtr's forge, furnace
hot and birthing
rock, glowing amidst
the melting bergs;
floating raft
of liquefied island
embryo.

III.
Seabird sanctuary,
puffins witness
one green shoot,
springing
from cooled
magma. Chicks
are hatched
and waves begin
to feast
on tephran beaches.

IV.
Solitary, Nordic,
dying from
the moment
of conception;
colonizers cling
to temporal
volcan rookeries.

On Friday Mornings I Watch Them Take the Trash Away

From windows spotted
with spray from washing
dishes, I watch this terrestrial
barge. From its stern swoop
men with dirty hands, they
grab my trash, dump
it in with everyone else's,
toss the empty bin into the yard
and climb back into the rigging,
sailing off to homes unknown.

They know not what they take,
these human turkey buzzards.
They take away my poop-
stained baby wipes, my boxes
with uneaten pizza crusts, my
tissues full of day-old tears,
memories that have passed
their expiration date. Senseless
melancholy—I miss those
unreadable memoirs.

On Saturdays I Mow the Grass at Pleasant Hill Cemetery

I hear voices beneath
these stones, faint over the helicopter
roar of the mower. German
Primitive Baptists, descendants of Welsh
miners, seven last names between
the twenty-six rows. I mow the outer edge

first, coming toward the graves in concentric
spirals, closer to the death and further
from the minutiae of manicured turf. I near
the stone of Ezra Hite, a father and husband
who, according to engraved rock, was loving.
Of course, he could have been an alcoholic

pedophile. Don't worry,
he's family—I'm allowed to say it.
He died in 1942 at the age of eighty-six,
father of at least eight who are buried
around him, lined up like stars
in a constellation I can't distinguish. But I never
can figure out stellar forms either;
I've never seen Ursa Major—or Minor,
I just see a bunch of lights.

Among limestone, granite, and marble,
blades whirr like rotor tails chopping turf
into an earthy slaw. I've chipped
four blades on one stone: a limestone square,
six by six inches, marked T.H.
For such a small marker it sure does
a lot of damage. I take off my shirt, hoping
the neighborhood girls will ignore my protruding
ribs and shoulder blades that look like

gargoyle wings. I toss it beneath the oak
whose roots have spread and corrupted half
a dozen graves, stones angled and raised
like rolling ships in a painting—the kind
where the waves are high, the sky
dark with clutching clouds, and the ship
in imminent danger of capsizing.
The kind of picture that hangs
in the Sunday School Room of the Thurston
Primitive Baptist Church.

Among these resting places of strangers, I pass
the stone of my great-grandma, interred
twelve years ago. She hasn't moved since. Not
that she moved much before we placed her
here. Her last five years she sailed through shoreline
fog without compass, sexton, or chart, her mariner
skills greatly diminished. In the end she fed
a stuffed cat named Otto cafeteria sloppy joes.
Otto was her husband, buried alone
for seventeen years until she joined him, although
she was probably mad about being put on the wrong
side of the bed. He was deaf in his right ear.
So am I—but it's not hereditary.

I stop for lunch, sitting on the slab that marks
the grave of David Llewellyn. On the headstone
of his wife, Amelia, I rest my ham and cheese
and Gatorade. A squirrel eats
a fallen nut from Abraham Hite's final resting
place. At least I'm not the only desecrator.

When I get up to resume my mowing,
I nearly trip over the stake near David's tomb

with the star and World War I insignia.
He didn't die at war, of course, or he'd be
a small white cross somewhere in France
or Belgium. No, he died in 1954, aged sixty. All
the veterans buried here died at home, boring.
Timothy Leary said dying is for squares. All
our circles eventually get flattened edges,
angular spherical cubes of life.

The sun is higher now, shadows falling across
these unintentional sundials—ancient astronomical
landmarks like some rural Ohio Stonehenge. Stones
once chiseled with expert precision, now smooth
in the insistent claws of an easterly wind.

I pass the mausoleum of the Wengetz family—separated
from the commoners even in death. They'd owned
the only bar in town for three generations. Paul
finally died in 2003 and the bar closed down. Old-timer
drunks still come to the tomb at night and raise
a bottle of Black Label in tribute to the ones who
fed their habits, dulled their fear and quieted
their wives. Old Moses Glynford preached
for years at camp meetings and railed against
bars and brothels and gambling dens. Now
his withering flesh and pock-marked bones
sleep in the shade of the big stone columns
and seraphimmed roof.

The mowing done, I turn to my weed-whacker
and move in close to stones so brittle that the string
of my trimmer eats away at their edges like frayed
page-ends of an old book. In the field

I glimpse a diving red-tailed hawk. It comes up empty-taloned
and vacant-beaked but returns unfazed to its perch

on the church's cable wire. Patrick O'Toole, this plot's
only Catholic, adrift in a sea of dead Protestants, lies
on the outer edge next to his Calvinist wife Sue.
She had always said that Pat would be in Heaven
regardless of what he or the Pope said, as long as God
willed it. Who knows, she'd say, maybe he'll be
there sipping wine with Christ and I'll be fanning
myself in Hell. If God wills it, of course, it will be.

Along the creek beneath the trees
are the unmarked graves of prisoners from the old
town jail. Discarded acorn caps and chestnut husks
left to rot somewhere between the silage
of life and the compost of death. I move
swiftly by these outposts of failure, barely trimming
the dandelions that cling to their blank slats.

I pause today as I do every week before the stone
of Melchior Brenneman. Inscribed by steady hands
it reads, "Time is but an illusion to the follower of Gob."
I wonder at the followers of Gob and I imagine their secret
rituals, like Masons on peyote. But then my trimmer
sputters and stops and Gob is left behind for gas.

I'll soon be leaving this place but am destined
to return. Here my grandparents rest and
here my parents will soon lie mute and cool;
I will follow after. Then someone else
can mow this plot of ground or I will sow it
with salt myself and go happily into the bald soil.

I don't like thinking these mowing thoughts,
so I turn to thoughts of soccer and babies
and double cheeseburgers. Leaving the cemetery

I glance back and notice a patch uncut. I leave
it to grow among those whose age has stopped.

Stepping Over Our Bodies

> *"If they come for the innocent and do not have to step over our bodies, then cursed be our religion."* —Dorothy Day

No, thank you, I can
walk just fine. I was just
resting. Don't step
over me, I can see
up your shorts—it's
unbecoming. Please, sir,
let me help you,
Sabine women must
be heavy. Why would
I mind? No, no, don't
eat that head of grain. It's for
the aliens.

Speaking For My Grandfather

If my grandfather came upon me
like the Holy Ghost whispering
mystery into Moshe's ear,
I know what he would say.

He would grab me and speak
his nonsense words—squeech,
kavoof—and sayings that
were pure original—b'ess heart
and bite nose. Then everyone
would know that I had been
indwelt by Grandpa's singular
spirit.

He would laugh and joke through
me, but beneath it all would
be words born of a much-lived
life—one with blood pumping
through two artificial valves.
When your heart clicks instead
of thumps, your words just
sound different.

Why I Hate Nasal Discharge

Today I blew my nose. I never
blow my nose—it's gross and nothing
ever comes out. But today into the kleenex
came a trickle of blood, followed by a stream
of twenty-seven-year-old amniotic fluid.
Next, a gush of learned behaviors and a torrent
of instinct. And then, finally, came
the lining of my nasal passage and clots
of God. I felt another bulge
of drying deity within my left nostril
but I left it there to harden and dam up
the rivers of dripping psyche. I sniffled escaping
theology and hoped it wasn't swine flu.

Where, Oh Death

Today I watched a man die.
It was my first time.

I didn't even know when
he had gone. I stood there
with thirty family members, praying.
We cried and hugged and left
and all along I wasn't sure if the man
in front of me was dead or alive.

He died before amen.
Thank God for context clues. So
I gave comfort and prayers, then
went home

where I read Lake
Wobegon Days and The
Gift of Good Land
and watched Villanova
beat Pittsburgh.

Wisps of Something More Than Smoke

I hear your oracle from depths
of cedar and oak; I glimpse you
translucent through screens
of burning bark.

I am the smoke from
this altar I've built for you; always
shifting, never constant. I'm
more pungent when fueled
by feral tares.

I am your hooded
priest atop a desolate
ziggurat; a naked
hermit perched upon a tower
in the desert. I am a celebrant
who dares not enter
the room behind
the curtain, where incense
rings your throne.

If you are the flame,
I am the haze rising from you.
If you are the waterfall, I am
the mist. How can the ashes
understand the fire?

And yet I see you when I see
her. Behind the shield of dream
filled infant eyes, I glimpse
the smoldering orbs of God.

Sitting on the Deck With Ranger Rick

This morning I attempted to connect
with nature—I threw a tomato
at a squirrel. Of course, I missed.
The little tree-rats were scurrying
and jumping off trunks like
so many capoeristas and nothing
short of an atlatl would suffice
to make my half-ripened fruit connect.

Out of ammunition, and unwilling
to pluck any more of my cherry
tomatoes from their umbilical
vine, I sat and surveyed the
squirrels. Thirty or so cavort among
the chestnuts, barking like bushy-tailed
dogs, lithe and agile and aggressively
cute. It's the cuteness that makes me
want to go and get

another tomato. But I don't. I just
sit there and watch and wonder
why God made squirrels. Upon further
reflection, I'm glad He did. It helps
me improve my aim.

A Moby Dick Kind of Sadness

I cannot go to sea, for
I cannot swim.

Still, whenever I find myself drowning
in the melancholia that comes from
finishing a good book and when I get
the urge to eat said book to ingest
all of its vital proteins and carbohydrates
and adverbs into my gerund-starved
digestive tract;

whenever I get the urge to lock
my keys in my running car and stay
in bed while the gasoline is all used up
and I am stranded here with my yellow
legal pads filled with mediocre lines;

whenever the first cool breeze
of autumn blows through my thinning
hair and the leaves of summer begin
to fall and I wish to hijack Thor Heyerdahl's
raft and sail to Raratonga Atoll;

and especially whenever I get the urge
to flee to the ridges and live the life
of a monastic hermit but instead
begin the work of fifteen different
unfinished novels, plays, and poems—

I realize that it is time to lie in bed
with you, to eat donuts and talk
about things you care nothing about
and to smell the hair of a baby.

The Mist Beneath Eagle's Rock

Ohio weather, indecisive
clouds, hot soil watered
by September, vapor massing
forces on the border,
granite and pine shrouded
in evaporated moisture.

Old-timers say that mist
is always in these hills;
my grandpa told me
the clouds were smoke
from squirrel campfires.
I told my friends that

and they laughed. I
laughed with them.
Now the storyteller's
gone and the mist
remains and the scent
of burning acorns still
mixes with the petrichor
of a Blue Valley autumn.

Speaking for the Mayan Dead

> *"We are not myths of the past, ruins in the jungle or zoos. We are people and we want to be respected, not to be victims of intolerance and racism."* —Rigoberta Menchú

We are no museum
pieces, no characters
in a Mel Gibson movie;
we are human flesh
and Mayan blood.

Tikal fell and Yucatan
jungles crept in with
all the furtiveness of
B'alam the jaguar,
but we clung to tropical

vines, ruins forgotten
in the quotidian struggle
to survive. Freed from
Xibalban fear, made
captive to foreign

lords; civil wars,
insurgencies, fought
with AK-47s and machetes
instead of jaguar-toothed
clubs and poison darts.

We read Subcomandante Marcos
instead of the Popol Vuh,
with lips still moving in
K'iche'. From this thin,
oft-burnt soil we wait

at the gates of Xibalba—at least
they will let us in.

Love Poem, Translated From the Banzakarian

Killdeer cry
for eggs lost
among the gravel.

I surround
their nest with bricks
and the killdeer cries
no more.

I'll surround
you and never
cry again.

Lakeside

From rocky shores we watched
sailboats on the lake. We walked
down Plum Street and laughed
at old men playing with sticks
and discs and wearing their
elastic bands to ward off
shuffleboard elbow. Two miles from
Marblehead, in the last of the
Chautauquas, we played
shuffleboard unprotected.

Dear Thief

To the schmuck who stole my GPS on Thanksgiving night

You're never going to read this.
I'm going to assume you're not the poetry type.

You're the type who is thankful for unlocked
doors and window mounts, for backlit screens
and morons like me who forget things. While I
tryptophaned from two dinners, valiant turkeys
reassembling inside my stomach, you were Plymouth
rocking me. Good luck finding where you're going;

satellites position cars and vans and hikers,
but thieves need more than orbitals.
You could have just asked for directions.

From Off the Western Coast

> *"Mochtili vun-machalan i'aj rojepp ni."*
> *[Remember the fruit bats; their turds become trees.]*
> —Banzakarian proverb

When the night herons are still
awake I go out to the marsh
and stare at the rook-leafed oaks.

Exiled in this land renowned
for its tin
cans and cotton
blends, I can see the pillar
cloud that marks the coast
and watch the gulls fly back
with bits of home
in their digestive tracts.

Convicted of sojourning (mobile vagrancy)
and accused of the desire
to roost in familiar branches,
sentenced to semi-soft labor
and a steady diet of poplar bark
and cream cheese, left alone
to revelate, to proselytize
the terns and kittiwakes,
to plot a return to nomad-guarded
shores.

Today I saw a sprout of Banzakarian fig
springing from the droppings of a flying fox.
I'll not be around to taste its fruit,
but someone will eat fecal-grown figs
and never know their origins.

Holy of Holies

Although
I always knew
the origins of rain,
I never told anyone.
Some things are too sacred.
Like watching drops bombing
from blitzkrieg skies where the sun
curtains through fog and you know
that above the clouds it is
not raining.

In Remembrance of Robert McNamara

I wonder what Robert McNamara thought
when that Quaker
set himself on fire within
view of the secretary's
Pentagon window, flames
licking and hissing like
Moshe's staff. I wonder
if he paid any attention to
Woodstock, if he ever
heard Country Joe McDonald
and the Fish sing
the Fixin' to Die Rag. I wonder if he
cheered Pete Townshend when he
guitar-slapped Abbie Hoffman
and drove him from the stage.
I wonder if he ever talked
to ghosts—the Kennedys,
Johnson, Westmoreland
and LeMay.

I wonder what Robert McNamara thought
when he stood before God
and saw that God
was Vietnamese.

The Poet

He smells like rain
and cedar smoke, he steps
with feet so recently bathed
in the trauma of sidewalks
and the illegitimacy
of jaywalking. He has
no clue where he's going
or why he's going there
and neither do I. But he smells
like fallen water—drops
that once touched clouds
and the forehead of God.

The Poet Identifies Beauty

I see beauty in the grass
of my front yard, wind-
blown blades that break
in waves from the street
to my front porch. They bend
and bow like ocean tides,
like forest canopies swaying
before the breeze, like rock
rippled pond waters. Or perhaps
I should mow more often.

I see beauty in the tree
that stands at the corner
of my house—its wicker
branches that reach into
the cable line and its leaves
that hide nesting birds
who are killed by cats and left
in the backyard for me
to mow over. But that
is not the tree's fault. Or perhaps
I should have dug it up before
the roots corrupted
our sidewalk and cracked
our basement wall.

I see beauty in the rain
that drops from pencil-shaded
clouds upon our yard. From
water-spotted windows I
watch the grass grow summer
green and admire the pattern
of falling drops. But then I pay
my flood insurance and mop
the water that comes through
the crack in the basement.

Observing a Polynesian Face Tattoo

Swirls that eel around eyes
and dots where teeth
of baleenic combs punctured
cheeks and flesh and drew
blood and constellations,

arches and sperm whale
fins, octopus discharge, quills
of the giant moa, petrified
and turned to wood,

moai blessed, tapu
guarded, shark followers
and water feelers, myth
tellers and spots that lore
the face with legends

Mai ho'oni i ka wai lana malie

Still this face charts foreign
seas; no home islands are found
amidst these shoals of cheekbones
and orbital sockets. Ink
blot constellations only reflect;
there's no navigation here.

Standing Atop Mt. Pleasant, August 26, 2009

> *"The work goes on, the cause endures, the hope still lives, and the dream shall never die"* —Ted Kennedy

No rainy morning with wasp
stings falling from sentinel clouds,
only early luminous sunbeams
peeking over the top of Mt. Pleasant.
Another day of alarms and baby

cries and dirty diapers. Another
day to go to work and wish for
self-employment. Today I sit
at the summit of the sandstone
cliff and watch the town below,

cars trundling like rhino beetles
across a land bowled out
by an ancient glacier. Ridge-encircled,
I call in sick for the day in favor
of communing with God

and the city of Lancaster. Round
bumps in the distance, geologic
warts, romanticize my thoughts
until I don't know whether to keep
crying or start smiling. Here,

Grandpa seems close. Among
sedimentary outcroppings
the immortal dream lives on.
And the view snatches
what's left of my breath.

Upon Hearing a Train

I heard a train last night, a little
after one. Its coyote-call
whistle conjured up vagrants
and sojourners riding
in empty boxcars, cattle-catchers
on the front of locomotives,
and the commemorative caboose
in Sugar Grove—a museum
that no one visits.

But upon hearing the nocturnal
call of freight in transit
I'm left with the feeling that deep
thoughts about locomotives do not
make me an engineer.

The View from Síocháin Díthreabhach

From these windows all I see
are corpse-pale bluffs of chalk
and a belligerent sea. The panes
mist with the spray of nautical
combat and vision blurs.

Outside all is shimmering in shades
of Xibalban gloom, but inside I
rest in the glow of things not real.
They shine in shadowy brilliance
and the window-mist no longer matters.

Thoughts on Neda From Deer Creek State Park

We entered the lodge on Sunday
afternoon, greeted by a sign—"Deer
Creek State Park welcomes
the Libyan Doctors of North America."
Five miles east of Pancoastburg,
on the shores of a dam-created
lake—apparently the hub
of North African expat medical
practitioners.

A king-size bed, a well-furnished
room, a fridge stocked with freshly
expressed breast milk—feels
like home. And then an olive-skinned,
turbaned man walks past me asking
the waitress if they serve bazin.
They don't.

In our room the baby poops
all over the paisleyed bedspread.
The room now smells of freshly
processed breast milk and I
turn on the TV for a distraction.
There, recently pumped plasma
pools beneath an unveiled
woman. Blue jeans and black
tee—a cleric's nightmare.
I've watched Neda die
at least fifteen times, blood

escaping through mouth and nose
and chest. It brought me to
tears a couple of times but
the baby just pooped again—third
time today. The Libyan doctors
are gone, still no bazin,
Neda remains dead and we
are going home.

Kuka'ilimoku

Slate skies dropping ashes from cigarette
clouds—prayer to a wood-carved god, prayer
to an unpronounceable tiki—I almost died today—
thoughts of Ku battling in Menehune valleys—my life
a shark-toothed knife, my world a lagoon,
a fish pond—you, a tidal surge that brings
new water to both—car skidding on pillows
of snow, unbrakeable, phone pole
accelerating—taking down your teak-wood body
I gaze into your empty eyes, once components
of a tree trunk—vacant, estuary-still, a wild
tuna tangled in torch-lit nets, long dead—your teeth
grimace-carved, your hair taro-long,
your hands full of weapons of war and shavings
of bark—a preacher with pagan thoughts,
I put you back, say a real prayer, and go back out
into the storm.

Centralia, PA

Walk these abyss-mouthed streets that smell
of liquified asphalt. Go past the caverned-in crossroads
where the stoplight long ago greened down
into bituminous slag. Mine the alleys for dead
canaries and compressed fish remains
from the late Cretaceous, feel the pull
of taffy-tar sinkholes, watch the house
on the corner of Main and Wallace

smolder from a fire set beneath the foundation.
Pay your respects to disappearing gravestones,
bodies mahogany-wrapped for safe keeping
until the Rapture, now cremated
and unfit to meet sky-appearing deity.
As steam vapors from fault-lined highways
kneel at St. Joseph's and petition all the Celtic saints
for mine shaft intercession. Beware

the sinkholes—there's flame underneath;
the deeper the mine the longer the burn.

Malagasy

You'll hate Antananarivo. You'll leave
as soon as you can. You'll search for
the highlands; not the bald ones, not the ones
painted with ochre and fresh mud,
not the ones where the fossas scour
the ruined ferns for carcasses of birds
who ran out of places to land.

You'll find that sea-sentral ridge
that smells of rain and tide and loam
and you'll sifaka from branches seasoned
with sea salt. And yet, from these feral
child beaches, you'll begin lusting
for the Maldives.

Inside the Chu Pong Massif

Binocular the forests from insurgent
tunnels, let your nostrils burn
with forty-year-old defoliant. Watch
water nymphs emerge from the Drang
and say a prayer before an altar

built to Tran Hung Dao. A rusted
bugle inscribed in French, a canister
alive among the dead, the droppings
of a muntjac—fortifications now defending
jungle ridges and Montagnard huts.

Lift into helicopter skies, long silent
to rotors that wasped through
moist air; move on to the next battlefield.
Whatever you're searching for,

it's not here.

Night in the Uncharted Territories

Come look for me tonight. You'll find
me where the coffee stains
the map a dusky sienna, crispy
and dry and fault-lined. I'll be somewhere
beneath the yurt-roof sparkling with bits
of silica, the pantheon of rotting
flesh from the Fertile Crescent, where the periodic
table contains Js and the Nile fits in
with the other rivers. I'll be with
the beautiful nocturnals neo-paganing
around mollusk-shell totems. The password
is one of the Eskimo words for snow.
We'll meet at the spot
where the Solutreans dropped
their fluted arrowheads before seeking
warmer weather in New Mexico. I'll be clovis

    pointing toward the horizon where dogs
    travel in herds and packs
    of cattle patrol the outskirts, picking
    off the stragglers. When you join
    me, pick the right word for snow.
    It has to be a wet kind, almost
    a slush—the snow that falls in spring
    when winter sneaks back into the woods
    disguised as a dying stag, antlers
    stained with cranberries and bleached
    white like a fallow deer. Don't forget

the rebels hold the hills
and hollows and have hidden
the maps of the liberated territories.
They have a different password.
Your mine is as good as a guess.

If I'm unfound, just stare
at the rivermouth, when the luna
fades to shades of songbird
eggs—you'll find a feather stuck
in the collarbone of an otter
and know that I am still exploring.

The Ingredients of Lake Air

Pungent your nose from a cottage
porch, beneath arbors of oak
and clouds of evaporated tides.

Drink the nectar of returned
water, steam your face with asphalt
vapor, indulge in the odor of death

from fish and rotting
seaweed. Smell the pier—its barnacled
posts and sweet fragrance

of waterlog. Watch the gulls
until you forget what inland
smells like. Then go home

and long for water, walk
by puddles and hear the waves,
see rain approaching and allow

the stored scents to baptize
you into memory and longing.

Eschatologically Speaking

What if I leave behind only
a femur—a clue
left for future generations to
misassemble? No skull to indicate
brain size and no skin or tissue
for context clues—only one
slim and fossilized orphaned
bone. Some still-to-come
paleontologist would puzzle over
my life and times and wonder
what I was and what I did. They
might think me some holy
man and treat my fossil
as a sacred antiquarian
relic. But what good would
that do me? I'd still be
just a femur.

Maybe they would label it
a spine and textbooks would tell
future students that I was a
stumpy sort of pre-hominid
with hair over ninety percent
of my body who made
Flores Man look like
Australopithecus. Jerks.
Perhaps they would treat
my thigh bone as some Mesozoic
artifact representing the upper
wing of the largest
known two legged bird.

My descendants would gawk
at my femury skeleton,
with its one real bone
and the rest made of
plaster. It would look nothing
like me. It might look
better.

The Habits of Ohio Waterfowl and Fifteen-Month-Olds

Eighty-seven hundred and seventy-two
steps around the pond at Cenci Park,
pushing your stroller—you, head-slumped, asleep,
not noticing mallards and geese fighting
over stale bread thrown from grubby hands
of six-year-olds. I look at this pond
with its duck-flap divots, circles of wingtip
tides. I brush the hair out of your eyes,
pull your hat down over your forehead
and protect your skin, creamy
like your mother's. You sleep-sigh and rub
a heavy eye, sailing back into dreams
of waterfowl winds and sun-reflecting
waters. I lose count of my steps and start over.

A Prayer for Peace

When Peace comes it will bring
a thousand sprigs of baby's breath
and the scent of departed rain.

When Peace comes we will find
that the hole in Heaven has been patched
with thatch from an Amazon hut;

we'll excavate dove-pecked bones
of Ottomans from the beaches
of Gallipoli; ptarmigans will roost

in cedars and baby otters will hide
from a predatory partridge; life
will cease to matter once war

slinks off to sulk in the desert
south of Khartoum. When Peace comes
we'll nomad off to Athabaskan plains

and dry our meat on racks of log-
cabin planks; the sun will wink
and the stars will stare and the prophets

will be released from their cisterns; war
will leave the dunes and sit alone on a bench
in Central Park. When Peace comes we'll bathe

in estuary mud; we'll satellite in search
of gladiatorial games or genocides; we'll
mourn while marching over the carcasses

of famined condors. When we study
war no more we'll mar the margins
of Homeric texts with dirty limericks

and rhymes about Pangur Ban. When
Peace comes we'll shelter ourselves
in stone-seated tunnels beneath school cafeterias

and plot the revolution.

Assiniboin Dead Perched in Boughs of Lodgepole Pine

South of the flat banks
of the Saskatchewan, amidst
the poplar and birch,
they rest in coniferous
solitude. Elemental
return, a burial at
tree, they watch over the groves
and the hills and the coyotes.

In night-dark dreams I see
these warriors of the pine,
Stone Sioux of the wooded
prairie—courageous, lying
exposed to the vulture
and the puma and the Crow.

I've studied them for
years, starting with
Where the Buffalo Begin,
then turning to Dee Brown
and books as thick
as Gall's chest. Among
the lodgepoles I remain
a quaking aspen, stuck
on this forest floor among
the cowards and the apathetic
and the apostate.

Stars are Pretty

We all know stars
are not dead
ancestors wandering up
the Milky Way to a nocturnal
paradise. They do not
watch us from Babelish
heights, twinkling their
approval. They are molten

balls of gas—a rocket blaster
odyssey away. No fireflies
trapped against an inky
canvas—only suns orbited
by unseen planets.

And yet on solitary nights,
hilltop gazing, I cannot
help but see Grandpa watching
from this planetarium dome.
Firefly bulbs twinkle
and my chest aches
from the tug of their gravity.

Sans

I glimpse her, afternoon moon pale
and crying Atacama tears. She walks
everyday up the hill on Broad Street,
minus a bra, teeth, and grace. I wonder
if she is anything like Mary Toft, giving
lagomorphic birth and mothering
lapine legs and bits of stew stock.
She seems kind of crazy like that.

She's old and frail and yet seems
to always be walking that hill
no matter when I pass by. It's almost eerie.
She slogs up toward High Street, pausing
for mocking orange hands or words
that tell her not to walk. But she still does.

I wonder if she's ESL, maybe originally
Faroese. I'll bet she lost her teeth
in a wild finback accident—that's how
she lost her husband. Aric had been a good
provider, but he shouldn't have pulled
out in front of a runaway whale
with bad brakes.

I can't look away. Then she Morrigans
me and I rear end the Taurus whose brake lights
are too small. The policeman doesn't believe
in witches. He writes me a ticket and, just
for good measure, searches my car.

Of Ba'al

After Tina Kelley

Ba'al is a concept.
Ba'al is to be continued.
Ba'al is etcetera.

Ba'al is easy to conjugate.

Ba'al is igneous and obsidian.
Ba'al is ash that turns to glass in the turbines of 757s.

Ba'al is the torch-tailed foxes that comet your fields.
Ba'al is the salt that Carthages your fields.

Ba'al is the melancholy of man-made lake floors.
Ba'al is the part that dreams of hoof prints and photosynthesis.

Ba'al is the guy that slows down when he sees the cops, even
    though he's driving the speed limit.
Ba'al makes slow right turns.

Ba'al is a sunset.
Ba'al is so cliché.

Ba'al is the poem you wish you'd written;
    the words you wish you hadn't said;
        the line you wish you'd remembered but forgot.

Ba'al is not here to take your call right now.
Ba'al is sleeping. Or on the toilet. Or asleep on the toilet.
Ba'al is graffiti on the rubble of Jericho.

Ba'al can never find the sock that goes missing in the dryer.
Ba'al knows how many licks it takes to get to the center of a
    Tootsie Roll Pop.

Ba'al never celebrates Mother's Day.

Ba'al is the one who invented the Omphalos hypothesis.
Ba'al is at the gates.
Ba'al moved to the midwest, changed his name to Walter, and
    now sells paint.

Ba'al is the gull that shows up fifty miles inland.
Ba'al is random smells that remind you of crushes, landmarks,
    and bodies of water.

Ba'al is.

When Bonhoeffer Hung Naked

Balding, pudgy, possessing
that German physique, sentenced
to die unclothed, without glasses,
alone. Flossenbürg's gallows
groan beneath the weight of Christ's
pacifist warrior. This peace-teaching,
would-be assassin—contradiction
swinging from knotted rope—mountain
top sermons expounded and the cost
of discipleship is the sum of
all the parts. Days from
liberation, he hung like some
butchered Black Forest boar.

They came three days late; or
maybe four years.

Poems Written on Leaves

I.

The first leaf only said "Peace"
but it fell and was erased
amid the communion wafer
grass of August.

II.

September leaves fell
and were burned and ashed
and cast into the air
like burning documents
at the Soviet embassy.

III.

Long after our highways
have quainted into stagecoach trails
leaves will still fall to defeated
angel earth. Satan awaits
the windswept and rain-pelted.

IV.

Behind the roadkill truck
on state route 37, contents
one rump-half deer
one whole whitetail minus sawed-off antlers
one car-hit coyote
one shell of raccoon exploded in autumn sun
one mound of decaying

leaves and mystery
fur. Where does it go?
Roadkill Valhalla, where the dead
rise to be hit again then feast
on unharvested corn and field mice.

V.

Ruins are no longer suitable
for human habitation. Now piles
of October rake these stones
and loam ancient kivas.

VI.

Falsetto these winds and sing
the song of autumn. I'll take the bass
on the chorus of the autumnal equinox
and we'll sing hallelujah
in the key of November—minor
and full of sharps.

VII.

Underground,
mind the gap.
Watch as rain drives
piles of petrichor
and tree-waste
into the sewer
of modern transport.

VIII.

Salmon on an icthyo-hajj
pause to genuflect beneath
rafts of treedeath and teeth
of leaf-tipped ursas.

IX.

When skin peeled away like Chrysanthemum petals,
when Icaran wings molted from lone bomber skies,
when Lucifer and his angels fell, watched through the sights
    of a B-52,
when Tsutomu Yamaguchi felt inferno in two doomed cities,
when the last leaves mixed with the ashes of samurai and
    Shinto shrines,
the trees surrendered their arms.

X.

The capital of Burkina Faso
is Ouagadougou; I've known that
since seventh grade but never
was able to use it until now.
Kids were jumping into piles
of leaves and I was inside,
studying geography
by the third floor window.

XI.

I'm not trying to be obstructionist,
but I'll poem this filibuster
and we can all leave for the Seychelles
and join bandoleered Somalis
who attack battleships on skiffs
and dinghies and never worry
about autumn.

XII.

My daughter's tears moved
like leaves but I told her
that only brown and blue
are permanent.

XIII.

Inscribed on the last leaf
in wrinkled, cracked deciduosity:
my mesophyll has forgotten
the photosynthian joys
of April.
Rake me,
burn me,
restore me to soil
and I will return through roots
so recently dangled from branches
damp with the mist of this valley.

Joe Inushiak

An Eskimo pothead, homeless
and headbowed from a collision
with a Jeep, as much a part of town
as the Nugget or the pink-brick
courthouse.

No Amaroq in him. Probably some
Aleut blood, prone to freezing at the high
latitudes. He dreamed of smoking some
with the Iditarod champ. One evening
in a backroom (little more than a stable,
like the one where Jesus was born) he toked
from a bowl and scratched, "I heard
the champ is in town." Head down,
not noticing the champ was passing him
the bong. "Dude, he's right next to you."
Look of awe from downturned face, jaw
would have dropped if his chin
hadn't been resting on his chest,
he smiled and smoked and his face
could have melted the Bering.

He froze to death two months later.
The town finally built a homeless shelter
after they found him stiff as baleen
and chin frozen to chest by thirty-below
saliva.

They left him on the tundra outside
Nome and he fed the foxes
and a lone lobo. One night the Inuit
came and he entered the arctic atmosphere,
his ashes blended with stalks of hemp.

Barrier Islands

In shades of kiln dust,
in shades of August grass,
in shades of the plain of Megiddo,
in siennas both burnt and raw—
these eyes of terra cotta
soldiers.

We warriors
immobile, we mercenaries
rooted to home, we wild geese
wingclipped, we who guard
the arches of Banzakar
with wheelbarrows full
of dead leaves, flintlocks
slung over separated shoulders;
we wait for invasion.

No one ever comes. This lighthouse
never lights, this coastline
never receives the bones of ships
and sailors, only the occasional
orca-escaping elephant seal.
Their bark is haunted
by starving white-spot calves.
The ocean is nearly empty
and we are alone. Stationed
here, on barrier islands, not quite
home but not away—a fate
worse than exile. Exiles
can dream of home and believe
that it is worth returning to.

Exiles can picture a seal-full sea
and not worry about the orcas.
There is no truth
in exile.

Tell My Daughter That One Day I'll Die

She's one year old now, so tell her
a little later. Tell her that trees
are not immortal and that every year
all the hornets in their mud-daub nests
die. Tell her that hearts stop, blood
stops flowing through arteries
and veins, the salmon eventually
lose to the dams and the bears.
Tell her not to be mad at me—death
is no one's fault. Tell her that I'll think
of her at the end, right before I see
holograms of light and am reminded
of all of my sins. Tell her I'll make it
and that I pray she does too. Tell her
that I'm going to die. And that I'm not
looking forward to it. Tell her that I
just couldn't tell her. She'll understand.

Elegy for a Bengali Island

Son of typhoon, daughter of sand
and gravel and coral-spitting
fish, now submerged by rising
temperatures—I'll miss you.

We never really knew you,
your beach of Sundarban mud
and tattered flags, now we never
will. May you rest submerged

in peace. Long live peace.

The Mound Builders

Blessed are they who built
without ever seeing.
They whorled and swayed beneath effigy
skies, they had fourteen words
for the way the ground smells
after rain, they crossed over humps
on feet of clay and lilac, they only sang
in the key of E minor. They loved
math. Blessed were the isosceles,
their cosines were always prime,
they flew on kestrel trajectories,
their serpents were winged
with thistles and the sporic heads
of dandelions. Blessed are the Mound Builders.

They couldn't see their eggs or perfect
circles; God made them
too low to the ground.
They should have been giants.
They should have been born
on their mothers' shoulders.
They should have flown.
They should have had elongated necks.

Where have you gone, Mound Builders?
You who whistled ash, you who spread
your fields with the droppings of wolves
and baited your lures with the tip
of a viper's tongue, are you hiding
in the rain-dropped forest? Are you still

and frozen, mounded beneath newly-rained
soil? What does it smell like?
Which word is it?

Mound Builders, is it memories-of-sea?
Is it home-of-earthworms? Is it too-few-and-far-between?
Is it smells-worth-three-in-the-mulberry?
Is it smoke-of-underground-priests?
Is it home? Is it air-that-smells-of-above?

I'll not name it. Some things are best
left smelling of mystery and rain.

Tenebrae

I. Noon

Beneath an arm of cedar squats
a preening mallard. We walk with hands
entwined along the river. It whispers
to us, but we don't understand
because rivers don't speak
English. Through the oaks the paths
appear, illumined by smoky
spring-sun tendrils.

II. Dusk

On June the sixth, nineteen sixty-eight
Robert Francis Kennedy was pronounced
dead. The genuflecting mallard
paused as we trudged through and found
two paths overgrown with aggressive
grass and oak roots. With mist settling in,
your hand felt cooler.

III. Midnight

I walk along the river path, your
shadow my company. Beneath the cedar rests
a pile of luminescent feathers and bits
of tiny bone. All along the water's
edge, bank mud tugs at the soles
of my feet. Tonight the stars
and Saigon are falling

Squirrel Somewhat Dead

Tail still twitching, imaginary
power line balancing act, now straddling
double yellow.
Stupid squirrel. I can't stop
thinking about that tail.

For My Daughter, Fifteen Months Old

If I shuffle off down the hall
and end up somewhere in the suburbs
of eternity, I'd still have you—a shimmering
school of sardines, pelican pouched; pemmican
for my journey; spores and seeds saved
beneath Svalbard's tundra; breath-steam
of an Irish elk, blended into breeze; ogham
on stones in rural Wisconsin.

But to you I would only be Croatan
carved in swamp-tree trunk.

You'd look at pictures and recognize yourself.
You'd look in the mirror and see
only you. But I would be there.

I watch you sleep tonight then turn
to shuffle off down the hall.

The Dead of Beaumont Hamel

Before we Beothuked from Sommish
fields, churned with martial carts
and hemofertile, we walked
bay bluffs and heard stories of Madoc
and Brendan and the Earl of Orkney.
Once, we found tide-brought leviathan,
fragments of cetacean bulk and bits
of broken baleen and we thought
ourselves great hunters aboard the *Pequod*.

I remembered the whale and Starbuck
and I heard Algonquin winds whisper
in a dead language as we skraelinged
out of Beaumont Hamel.

Benediction

for Killian McDonnell

Triune God, when my
peregrine days are over
leave me to the taiga—it
doesn't judge.

From Baikal shores I'll punt
my raft, boreal banks
waiting to receive
this tiger-food flesh.

Kamchatkan comets
can burn the clouds
and I will remain entombed
above a baby mammoth,

well-preserved and whole.
Leave my body to be mortified
by sky-bound ravens
and call it theosis.

When We're Older We'll Buy a Cottage in Lakeside

Walking down leaf blanketed streets that slope
lakeward, an irresistable decline leading to boulder-lined
shore, passing these homes with plaques and signs,
named like pier-docked sailboats, arboreal yards
and leperous paint applied half a century ago;
over green-grey waters and beneath a gravel sky
seagulling past the shuffleboard courts.

In the tide-thick evening, porched behind
screens, rocking shared dreams in grooves
carved into astroturf floors; the wave-pushed sun
spots the dust that floats through the bedroom,
awake and lying on damp sheets, moist from
various stages in the water cycle—tree-caught dew
and drops of lake bound for cumulus shores, smelling

what remains of last night's petrichor, arms and legs
helixed, beginning another day of walking streets
once strolled by new parents, now paced by those
who have seen the future pass, realizing life
somewhere between the gate, the pier, and the gulls.

Lullaby

Dream dreams of dreaming—the ones
where you wake up and you're still
sleeping; the ones where you wake up
and wonder why the covers are wrapped
around your head like sarcophagal rags;
the ones where you wake up and wonder
why you're not sleeping next to a man
in a gorilla suit. Dream those dreams
and when you wake up tell me
what you saw. It's very important

that you tell me everything. Don't leave out
the exact smell of the rain. Was it mixed
with sassafras? Was it anointed
with oil? Did it smell like spring
lettuce? Melting summer asphalt?
Did it smell like deathbed
leaves? Don't leave out
the colors or the way the sounds
shook your ribs. Remember which ribs
shook. That's important.

Are you asleep yet? Don't miss
this part; you'll need it
when the dreams turn igneous
and craggy. Remember that sleep
is nomadic, dreams are yurts,
the herds are always moving on,
the dunes are always dancing.
If you see the gull-stained cliffs
know that it was a good dream.
Know that home has found your bed.

About the Author

Adam Hughes was born in 1982 in Lancaster, Ohio. He is a pastor and poet and has worked as a program director for individuals with cognitive and physical disabilities since 2007. His first chapbook, *Pilgrim Poems*, was released in 2010 by Pudding House Press, and his poems have appeared widely in print and online in journals such as the *New York Quarterly*, *Tipton Poetry Journal*, *The Foliate Oak*, and *West Ward Quarterly*. He resides in Lancaster with his wife and two-year-old daughter.

About NYQ Books™

NYQ Books™ was established in 2009 as an imprint of The New York Quarterly Foundation, Inc. Its mission is to augment the *New York Quarterly* poetry magazine by providing an additional venue for poets already published in the magazine. A lifelong dream of NYQ's founding editor, William Packard, NYQ Books™ has been made possible by both growing foundation support and new technology that was not available during William Packard's lifetime. We are proud to present these books to you and hope that you will continue to support The New York Quarterly Foundation, Inc. and our poets and that you will enjoy these other titles from NYQ Books™:

Barbara Blatner	*The Still Position*
Amanda J. Bradley	*Hints and Allegations*
rd coleman	*beach tracks*
Joanna Crispi	*Soldier in the Grass*
Ira Joe Fisher	*Songs from an Earlier Century*
Sanford Fraser	*Tourist*
Tony Gloeggler	*The Last Lie*
Ted Jonathan	*Bones & Jokes*
Richard Kostelanetz	*Recircuits*
Iris Lee	*Urban Bird Life*
Kevin Pilkington	*In the Eyes of a Dog*
Jim Reese	*ghost on 3rd*
F. D. Reeve	*The Puzzle Master and Other Poems*
Jackie Sheeler	*Earthquake Came to Harlem*
Jayne Lyn Stahl	*Riding with Destiny*
Shelley Stenhouse	*Impunity*
Tim Suermondt	*Just Beautiful*
Douglas Treem	*Everything So Seriously*
Oren Wagner	*Voluptuous Gloom*
Joe Weil	*The Plumber's Apprentice*
Pui Ying Wong	*Yellow Plum Season*
Fred Yannantuono	*A Boilermaker for the Lady*
Grace Zabriskie	*Poems*

Please visit our website for these and other titles:

www.nyqbooks.org

www.ingramcontent.com/pod-product-compliance
Lightning Source LLC
LaVergne TN
LVHW011424080426
835512LV00005B/261